WOMEN'S
RIGHTS
AND
THE LAW

FAITH AND FREEDOM
SERIES

WOMEN'S RIGHTS AND THE LAW

JOHN W. WHITEHEAD

MOODY PRESS
CHICAGO

For legal assistance or educational materials,
contact The Rutherford Institute at:

P.O. Box 7482
Charlottesville, Virginia 22906-7482
(804) 978-3888

* * * * * * *

ISBN: 0-8024-6690-7

1 3 5 7 9 10 8 6 4 2

Printed in the United States of America

From the beginning of time, the question of the proper roles and rights of women has been a source of confusion and concern. Each culture has struggled to find a workable answer. Without significant exception, the results have been to the detriment of the female.

Many contemporary Americans have grave concerns regarding environmental, property, tax, welfare, and business issues. Much attention is also paid to so-called women's issues, which include the foregoing but also encompass the profound issues of abortion, sexuality, equality in the workplace, education and homes, and sexual crime, oppression, discrimination, and harassment.

At the same time, modern America is confronted with families without fathers, teenage pregnancies and suicides, abused wives (as well as abused children, husbands, and elderly), adultery and other sexual encounters outside marriage, and all the other indicia of a society that has little idea of how to form or support the most basic of human relationships: that between a man and a woman.

Most would agree that this must be changed. Perhaps fewer would agree on the nature of such change.

Differing Solutions

German feminist Gabriele Dietze describes her view of what will be required to resolve the concern and confusion in modern Western society:

> No revolution in one sector alone—and certainly not an economic one only—can break through the complex system of the psychological, social and economic conditioning of suppression [of women by men]. Everything has to be changed: the way of thinking, the way of governing, the whole way of life, the family, how to go about one's work—the whole technical/economic complex—yes, how we laugh, love and cry, and even how we dream—all this has to be changed.[1]

Time magazine essayist Barbara Ehrenreich characterizes the problem—and thus the solution—differently:

> So we have, in the Susan Smith case, the female dilemma at its starkest: Not the pallid "family-vs.-career" predicament, but a zero-sum choice between romantic love and mother love, with guaranteed misery no matter which you chose. Novels like *Anna Karenina* taught us the "bad" woman's fate, which is ideally suicide. *The Bridges of Madison County* gives us the "good" woman's answer, which is to renounce romantic love for the sake of husband and kids. But the more dis-

quieting message of that story is that four days and three nights with a sexy stranger can outweigh anything else that ever happens in a "good" woman's life.[2]

Reflecting still another view, feminist leader Gloria Steinem reputedly coined the slogan "A woman without a man is like a fish without a bicycle," expressing the view that women are complete without men—and, by implication, complete without the roles and responsibilities that result from relationships with men. In this view, neither romantic love nor mother love are required by women for fulfillment or wholeness.

Still other feminists identify heterosexuality itself as the "enemy" and urge that women relate sexually—and thus most intimately—only to other women.[3] The theory is that this would eliminate subjugation of women through the elimination of patriarchal relationships.

Contemporary American Christians —women as well as men—are struggling with these issues as well. All too often Christians allow others to define which roles and rights are proper for women and their relationships to men and society, instead of examining the Bible to see the roles God has ordained for them.

Yet, the principles laid down by Jesus Christ and the New Testament writers nearly two thousand years ago provide the only authentic framework for relationships between men and women and the society and church in which they interrelate.

This framework must be established first in our marriages and then in our homes, our churches, and finally in our society. Only this will lead to the resolution of all the other issues that continue to trouble our societies to this day.

Indeed, the failure to understand the biblical model actually contributes to the problem. An example of this confusion may be seen in the debate about requiring welfare mothers to work. Proposals abound that would *require* "welfare" mothers to learn job skills and then to enter the workplace.[4] Yet, many of those who laud such requirements propose—at the same time—that non-welfare mothers should *leave* the workplace and return to their homes. The message delivered by these actions seems to be that "welfare" children do not deserve the benefits of a stay-at-home mother. This demeans not only mothers but also their children.[5]

A Christ-centered approach to this issue would include proposals that *elevate* both the woman and the mother in all situations and minimize those factors that devalue her. *Every* mother is a "working" mother.

This book will first review the basic principles given to us by Jesus Christ, as revealed in the biblical accounts of His teaching and actions. *Imago dei* is the key concept.

Second, a summary of the modern women's movement in America will be provided. Although important "women's liberation" movements have occurred and continue to develop throughout the world, the scope of this book does not encompass all such movements—or even the entire women's liberation history (or *"her*story," as some would say) in America.

Third, some of the current issues and legal rights relating to women will be summarized.

Finally, a conclusion will be drawn regarding the effect of our failure as Christians to reconcile the teachings of Christ with the roles and responsibilities of modern Christian men and women and the society in which we live.

The Christian Perspective

Throughout history, women have generally not been accorded the respect and status of men, even in societies that did not actively harm or persecute females. This is true in today's American society.

In the West, Christianity provided some relief for this cultural defect. However, some religious beliefs still limit a woman's sphere of influence to the home.[6] Some religious views impute value to a woman primarily on the basis of childbirth, child rearing, and homemaking. This view has pervaded Christianity from its beginnings through Augustine, Aquinas, and Calvin to present times.[7] Those who hold such views, however, should consider the model woman as presented in Proverbs 31, who is a wife and also ably conducts business.

More narrowly, few would dispute that the social and religious context of the Hebrew and New Testament cultures were patriarchal. Much of this context has been incorporated into Christian religious beliefs, including at subconscious levels, and has been applied outside its religious context to society as a whole. However, a true understanding of the message of Jesus Christ regarding the treatment of women (and other oppressed people, such as slaves and "foreigners") inevitably leads to the rejection of any *social* and *legal* patriarchy. Christ rejected the elevation of one social group over another. *Every* human being is created in the image of God and, thus, there is no Christian justification for the domination or subjugation of one group by another.

The male creation is not more God-like[8] than the female, and it could be said to be idolatrous to make men so. This is the clear message of Christ as He sought to free women from the various social and religious restrictions of His time. This is not to say that

Christ made a plea for androgyny or the blurring of gender differences, and none is made here. To the contrary, a key concept of true equality is the *respect for*, not *obliteration of*, differences.[9]

An important component of the radical feminist agenda today is "gender deconstruction." Simply put, this means that gender is a *state of mind*, not a physical characteristic. Societal —and religious—conditioning, so the theory goes, are the basis for one's sexuality. Thus, with gender deconstruction, the supposed "patriarchal" systems will no longer stand—because there will no longer be "men" who can be the patriarchs. *Everyone* can be men, or women, or both!

The deconstruction of gender is also intended to validate and normalize any and all forms of sexual expression and conduct—bisexual, homosexual, and heterosexual.

These concepts are in clear contradiction to scriptural principles. The key concept of *imago dei* is laid out in the Bible: "So God created man in His own image; in the image of God He created him; *male and female* He created them."[10] Also, "a man shall leave his father and mother and be joined to his wife, and the two shall become one flesh."[11]

Jesus Christ—one of history's greatest radicals—had a plan for a new spiritual order. This has social implications in that all of *man's* governmental and religious distinctions based upon sex, race, and class could be overcome in Christ. There would be neither male nor female, Jew nor Greek, slave nor free humans, insofar as their rights, roles, and responsibilities in society, under the law, and with respect to salvation and redemption from sin are concerned. Christ rejected the use of religion to institutionalize and sanctify hierarchies, except with the limited patriarchal system of the local church and the institution of the family.

The patriarchal design of the family and the New Testament church, however, does not mean that women are inferior to men. Nor does it mean that husbands are to establish dictatorships over their wives and children. Indeed, the command of Ephesians 5 is for the man to love his wife as Christ loved the church—a sacrificial love in which the husband is willing to forsake all for his spouse. God has assigned certain functions and roles within these fundamental institutions. Moreover, the patriarchal nature of the local church, for example, is no ground whatsoever to transfer the patriarchal concept to society as a whole. Christ's liberation principles in some ways, therefore, have a greater impact as they operate in society than as they function in relation to traditional religious structures.

Finally, Christ also rejected the use of His teachings to justify the revenge of the oppressed. The message of Jesus Christ is *not* simply to *reverse* systems of domination and repression. This means that those in today's society who seek to deny the value and uniqueness of the *male* also misunderstand the message of Jesus Christ as significantly as do those who oppress and subjugate women.

In the kingdom of God, there will be no domination and subjugation. And Jesus Christ prayed that God's will would be done on earth, as in heaven. The corruption of the liberating tradition of Jesus Christ must give way to a clear focus on social justice and the proper use of power and hierarchy.

If we are able to accomplish this, we can deepen our understanding of social sin and the revolutionary meaning of the teachings of Jesus Christ. The guidelines of Jesus Christ are clear and easy: Whatever diminishes the full value of any human is not Christian. Whatever promotes and supports the full value of any human reflects the full message of Jesus Christ that all humans are created in the image of God—and this includes women.

The Actions and Teachings of Jesus Christ

Jesus Christ saw worth in all humans. He came to earth to offer Himself as a sacrifice for all people. Thus, in at least one sense, He viewed all people as the same: candidates for salvation. As one author argues: "He dealt with Mary and Martha, Zacchaeus, harlots and tax collectors, fishermen and rulers of the synagogue as human beings, all in need of spiritual refreshment and growth."[12]

Moreover, because Christ became a man, He experienced the temptations and hardships all human beings face and thus was able to understand people and their daily trials and successes. As God, Jesus created people and loved them, and, free from sin, He was not tainted by the bias and prejudice that people have in general.

These truths explain Jesus' attitudes and actions toward *people*, women as well as men. As the apostle Paul states in Galatians 3:28: "There is neither Jew nor Greek, there is neither bond nor free, there is neither male nor female: for ye are all one in Christ Jesus." This was precisely Jesus' viewpoint, and He treated all persons accordingly.

As the writer Heinrich Böll states:

In the New Testament there is a theology of what I would dare to call tenderness, which always has a healing effect: through words, through the laying on of the hands, which one can also call caressing, through kisses, a meal together—in my view all this is totally destroyed and distorted by legalization, one might well say by the Roman approach which has made this into dogmas, principles and catechisms; this element in the New Testament, that of tenderness, has certainly not yet been discovered.[13]

In replacing legalities with tenderness, Jesus Christ sometimes violated the religious and cultural customs of the day. He offended the Pharisees on numerous occasions.[14]

Christ interacted with many women during the course of His life on earth. He and the disciples were ministered to by a group of women who traveled with them, which included Mary Magdalene and Joanna, the wife of Herod's steward.[15]

Moreover, some of His best friends were women. John writes that Jesus loved Mary and Martha.[16] The Gospels recount that it was women who first received the news of His resurrection, who first encountered Jesus after His resurrection, and who were commissioned to bring the news to His disciples. Therefore, in a sense, women were the first to tell the Gospel, the good news that Jesus was risen from the dead.

Through all these associations, Jesus showed His love for, high valuation of, and respect toward these women, all attitudes rarely seen in His time or, sad to say, even today in the church that supposedly practices the religion of Christ.

The devaluing of women must be corrected if we are to be truly Christlike. It can best be rectified by emulating the attitude of Jesus Christ toward women, as reflected in the manner in which Jesus dealt with women as recounted in the four Gospels.

Mary and Martha

Mary and Martha may have been the most important and prominent women in Jesus' life after His own mother.[17] They are featured in three major stories: (1) a tension between the two sisters over roles;[18] (2) the grief of the two sisters at the death of their brother Lazarus, who was then raised from the dead by Jesus;[19] and (3) the anointing of Jesus by Mary.[20]

The first story recounts the preparation of food by Martha while Mary is sitting at Jesus' feet and "hearing His word."[21] Jesus replies that, although Martha is concerned about many things, "Mary has chosen that good part, which will not be taken away from her."[22] Although the story's focus appears to be on the tension between Martha and Mary and Mary's choice of the "needful" thing, what is important for Christians to consider is *Mary's* behavior: Mary's choice was not a conventional one for Jewish women. She sat at the feet of Jesus and listened to "His word." This passage implies that Jesus was teaching her, giving her religious instruction. "Jewish women were not permitted to touch the Scriptures; and they were not taught the Torah itself, although they were instructed in accordance with it for the proper regulation of their lives. A rabbi did not instruct a woman in the Torah."[23]

Christ ignored these religious dictates and enabled women to interact with the Word directly. Essentially, this passage of Scripture "vindicates Mary's rights to be her own person."[24] In a sense, it gives women value apart from the tasks traditionally performed by women. These verses recognize the "full personhood of woman."[25]

The second story concerns the death and resurrection of Lazarus. Martha hears that Jesus is coming and goes to meet Him, confronting Him and stating that had He been there, her brother would not have died.

Jesus and Martha then discuss Jesus' deity, which is affirmed by her statement: "Yes, Lord, I believe that You are the Christ, the Son of God, who is to come into the world."[26]

This confession of Jesus' status as God is significant for various reasons. Only in one other instance in the Gospels does this occur, when Peter confesses Jesus' deity.[27] Also significant, Jesus confirms His own deity with the statement that He is "the resurrection and the life," thus prompting Martha's confession.

> By giving his audience a story in which a woman is the recipient of one of Jesus' most profound and direct statements about Himself, and in which a woman makes a heartfelt and accurate response to Jesus' declaration, the

Fourth Evangelist intimates that women have a right to be taught even the mysteries of the faith, and that they are capable of responding in faith with an accurate confession.[28]

All four Gospels contain a story of a woman who anoints Jesus. Because the passage in John is the only one to identify this act with Mary of Bethany, Martha's sister, the passage of John is examined here.[29] In these verses, Mary anoints Jesus' feet with perfume and wipes them with her hair. This is important for several reasons.

First, Mary showed great selflessness. She uses a large amount of expensive perfume, a pound of spikenard, thinking nothing of herself or the cost of the perfume. This is the complete opposite of the actions of Judas Iscariot, who focuses on the cost of the perfume and thinks only of the use of the money. "Mary's generosity is set off against his avarice, his pettiness against her large-heartedness."[30]

Second, Mary pours the perfume on the feet of Jesus and wipes it off with her hair: "That was the task of the lowliest slave: the master at the table used to wipe his dirty hands on the slave's hair."[31] However, here it is the ultimate act of humbling oneself before the Lord.

Third, Mary's act serves as a preparation for Jesus' burial, for the use of large amounts of perfume was identified with burial rites.[32] Thus, Mary may be the first, whether consciously or not, to acknowledge Jesus' purpose and future, that of dying, being buried, and rising from the dead. Mary's action stands in sharp contrast to the disciples' behavior.

> The men who have accompanied him from the early days have become increasingly confused and doubtful. They fundamentally misunderstand him. They cannot bring themselves to imagine that this hopeless revolution might end with suffering and death. They protest when Jesus speaks of his death (Mark 8:32); anxiety seizes them (Mark 10:32).[33]

Fourth, Mary shows courage that is lacking in the men around Jesus and embraces Jesus' death.

Fifth, Mary's action may also be seen as even more significant in light of its timeliness: It occurs shortly before Jesus' final journey into Jerusalem, where He will be condemned and crucified. Thus, this action was no doubt of great comfort to Jesus.

Sixth, her action can be paralleled with Jesus' washing of the disciples' feet one chapter later, in John 13. When Peter protests, Jesus replies:

> You call me Teacher and Lord, and you say well, for so I am. If I then, your Lord and Teacher, have washed your feet, you also ought to wash one another's feet. For I have given you an example, that you should do as I have done to you.[34]

In Luke, Jesus states during the Passover meal: "For who is greater, he who sits at the table, or he who serves? Is it not he who sits at the table? Yet I am among you as the One who serves."[35]

Jesus was the greatest servant ever to live. Second to Jesus, though, Mary exemplifies servanthood, with her anointing of Jesus' feet. A woman, not a man, then, serves and comforts Jesus as no other did and provides the greatest example of humbling oneself before the Lord.

The Samaritan Woman

Jesus interacted with other women, remaining consistent in His treatment of them. In one instance, Jesus asks for a drink from a Samaritan woman and talks with her, contravening the conventions of His religion. First, in asking for a drink from the Samaritan woman, Jesus surprises her because the code of purity forbade a Jew to eat or drink from a vessel of a non-Jew, as non-Jews were considered ritually unclean[36] (even though Jews had some interaction with Samaritans on a business level and otherwise).[37]

The fact that Jesus *spoke* with a woman is also significant. The disciples "marveled that He talked with a woman."[38] A man in the Jewish world did not normally talk with a woman in public, even his own wife. Moreover, Jesus' disciples referred to Him as "rabbi," and "rabbinic regulations were so strict that not even a rabbi was to speak to his wife in public."[39]

Additionally, the woman's personal life and history are noteworthy. For Jesus knew, as He tells her, that the woman had already had five husbands and was currently living with a man to whom she was not married.[40] It was Judaic custom not to have more than three marriages in a lifetime. Morally, more than three would be suspect. Moreover, living with a man other than her husband would make this woman ritually unclean.[41] Jesus had been attacked elsewhere for associating with sinners.[42]

Even though Jesus was perfect and this woman was far from being so, He did not choose to refrain from speaking to her. He saw all people as needing salvation and perhaps those considered as sinners more needful of His attention. As He said in Luke 5:31–32: "Those who are well do not need a physician, but those who are sick. I have not come to call the righteous, but sinners, to repentance."

Finally, the *results* of this conversation are important. Not only does the woman come to believe in Him, but she also brings many of her fellow Samaritans to Jesus, who in turn believe that He is the "Christ, the Savior of the World."[43] Thus, this woman, whom Jesus Christ was expected to ignore, in essence became an evangelist, leading others to Jesus. "Jesus liberated this

21

woman and awakened her to a new life in which not only did she receive but also gave."[44] He saw through her sin, her status as a woman, and her race to her personhood and, thus, saved her soul.

Jesus Christ, therefore, sets the foremost example for Christians. He defied not only the conventions and institutional religious practices of His time but also those of today. Unfortunately, the designations of race and gender, as well as the perceptions of one's spiritual status, still prevent Christians from reaching out to many. Jesus ignored those designations and perceptions and saw the Samaritan woman's value as a person, as He did all people, Jew or Samaritan, woman or man.

Challenging Hypocrisy

In some of His efforts toward women, Jesus also challenged the hypocrisy of the religious leaders of His day. Two examples occur when Jesus heals a woman "bent over"[45] and when a woman caught in adultery is brought to Him.[46]

In the latter instance, Jesus is teaching in the temple when the Pharisees bring before Him a woman caught in adultery. Quoting Mosaic law that the woman must be stoned, they ask Jesus what should be done. The apostle John states that they were testing Jesus, trying to trap Him.[47] Jesus simply challenged those who were without sin to throw the first stone. This convicted the Pharisees, and, confused, they all left His presence. Jesus, then, seeing that they were gone, questioned the woman and said: "Neither do I condemn you; go and sin no more."[48]

The Pharisees saw the woman only in terms of her sin, and for them she was just a means of accusing Jesus. "Her accusers were after Jesus, not just her. She was to them a worthless object to be used in trapping Jesus."[49]

On the other hand, Jesus recognized the woman as a person. He did not condone her adultery. Rather, He acknowledged that she had sinned and turned her in a new direction.[50] Christ encouraged her to admit her sin and turn from it.[51] "In this story, Jesus rejected the double standard and turned the judgment upon the male accusers. His manner with this sinful woman was such that she found herself challenged to a new self-understanding and a new life."[52] He recognized her as a person with a worth greater than her sin and enabled her to begin a new life.

The apostle Luke reports the story of a woman who had been sick for eighteen years and was "bent over," unable to stand up straight. She entered the temple on the Sabbath day, and Jesus healed her, angering the ruler of the synagogue, who remarked to the crowd that healing should not be done on the Sabbath. Jesus responded fiercely, calling the ruler a hypocrite, stating that although the ruler would water his ox or donkey on the Sabbath, he would prevent this woman, a "daughter of Abraham," from being healed. Luke then notes that all the adversaries of Jesus Christ were put to shame and the people rejoiced for all the glorious things Christ had done.

The significance of this story seems to lie not in the actual healing but in the statements of Jesus. For when Jesus first saw the woman, He said, "Woman, you are loosed from your infirmity" and then laid His hands on her, healing her.[53] Although Christ was obviously speaking of her disease, He may also have been alluding to another type of restriction. "In a real sense, Jesus has enabled women to stand up with a proper sense of dignity, freedom, and worth."[54]

This is further reinforced when Christ refers to the woman as a "daughter of Abraham." This title, while having been applied to Israel as a whole, had not been used previously to describe an individual.

Jesus, then, healed this woman of more than a physical ailment. He also sought to give her status as a person and, in doing so, freed the woman not only from a physical sickness but also a symbolic infirmity.

All Humans Are Valued Equally

The Bible shows that Jesus Christ related to women as persons of worth and dignity. He did not seek to abolish the system of patriarchy. Rather, Christ sought a system where all human beings, including women, would be valued equally. His dealings with women demonstrate that Christ considered them as possessing intelligence, capable of discussing theology and even debating, as Martha and the Gentile woman do. Women are capable servants of God, able to minister to fellow human beings and God. Jesus also dealt with women in a manner demonstrating that they possessed value in addition to the worth of the tasks they performed in the home.

Thomas Aquinas, thought by some to be "undoubtedly the most influential thinker in Christian history,"[55] stated that woman "is defective and misbegotten."[56] He saw her worth only in childbirth: "She was not fit to help man except in generation, because another man would have proved a more effective help in anything else."[57]

Some of these beliefs sound similar to ones reflected in many Christian circles where a woman's worth is defined solely by childbirth and the tasks of homemaking. Christians, however, should not follow the principles of Plato or Aquinas concerning women. Instead, Christians are obligated to worship Jesus Christ and follow His teachings, including those concerning women. Christ treated women as possessing value. He did not see them as property or merely in terms of what they could give Him.

Rather, Christ was willing to die on the cross for women and, as such, certified their worth with the ultimate selfless act.

The Modern American Feminist Movement

As in the time of Jesus Christ, modern women, men, and their societies struggle with the matter of women's roles and rights. Today's "feminists" concern themselves with topics ranging from governmental issues to employment discrimination.[58]

Carole King, an officer of the National Organization for Women (NOW), defined a *feminist* as:

> [A]nybody who will not tolerate being thought of as inferior to anybody else merely because of their body difference.[59]

Defined this way, little difference appears between the teachings of Jesus Christ and contemporary definitions of feminism. However, many of the goals and achievements of the more radical feminists are as antithetical to the teachings of Christ as the actions of those who subjugate and/or devalue women.

The Christian goal is to affirm the variety of God's creation without devaluing anyone. Ironically, many modern Christians and conservatives who decry the rise of radical feminism have their forefathers to blame. If the late eighteenth- and early nineteenth-century Christians had practiced true Christianity, the women's movement for equal rights would and should have been a true Christian movement.

Modern Feminist History

Recorded history has largely failed to reflect adequately the contributions of women, even in America. But as Irene Stuber, author of Netscape's *Women of Achievement and Herstory*, writes:

> Don't let anyone tell you there weren't notable and effective women throughout history. They were always there, but historians failed to note them in our histories so that each generation of women has had to reinvent themselves.[60]

Women made significant contributions to the founding of America. For example:

> We all know George Washington was with his troops during the long, cold winters. But not too many people know that Martha Washington was by his side and served as nurse and cook for the troops. When the war was over, Washington made an eloquent speech before Congress to acknowledge her contribution and award her a pension for her services.[61]

The scope of this book is too narrow to permit even a survey of these contributions. But a quick review of the modern American women's movement is important in understanding the cultural and religious milieu in which contemporary Christians find themselves concerning the rights and roles of women.

Betty Friedan and *The Feminine Mystique*

The modern women's movement essentially began in the late 1950s with the work of Betty Friedan and her 1963 book, *The Feminine Mystique*. In a 1964 speech given to the University of California at San Francisco, she said:

> I say that the only thing that stands in women's way today is this false image, this feminine mystique, and the self-denigration of women that it perpetuates. This mystique makes us try to beat ourselves down in order to be feminine, makes us deny or feel freakish about our own abilities as people. It keeps us from moving freely on the road that is open to us. It keeps us from recognizing and solving the small, but real problems that remain. . . . With little help from society, you have begun to make a new pattern in which marriage, motherhood, homemaking —the traditional roles of women—are merged with the possibility of women as individuals, as decision-makers, as creators of the future.[62]

Women began returning to college and seeking the careers they had thought impossible, often sacrificing finances and time spent with families to obtain independence. Other women retained the view that homemaking could still be an appropriate full-time career.[63]

Friedan urged women to recognize a "fourth dimension" beyond the three-dimensional relationships of mother, wife, and homemaker. She claimed that the "fourth dimension woman" encompassed obtaining a *fulfilling* job and being committed to that profession, being an accomplished volunteer, finishing or continuing a formal education, and turning "mothering" skills into professional endeavors, such as starting day camps or taking business advantage of cooking opportunities.[64]

Friedan eventually founded an organization "to take the actions needed to bring women into the mainstream of American society, now, full equality for women, in fully equal partnership with men."[65] This resulted in the birth of the National Organization for Women (NOW).

National Organization for Women

When NOW began on October 29, 1966, there were only about three hundred members present at the Washington, D.C., meeting.[66] NOW currently reports some 250,000 members and six hundred chapters in the United States. It supports extensive lobbying and political action, initiates litigation, and orchestrates a radical feminist agenda in pursuit of women's rights. It has organized mass marches, pickets, rallies, counter-demonstrations, and immediate, responsive "zap" actions.[67]

As a result of Friedan's zealous efforts for equalization in regard to women's careers, NOW became famous for its slogan Every Mother is a Working Mother and the phrase "women who work outside the home." In the 1970s, NOW's lobbying and picketing of local newspapers and its Equal Employment Opportunity Commission complaint forced newspapers to eliminate male-dominant help-wanted ads.[68]

NOW expanded its efforts to include women's economic rights (e.g., jobs, credit, insurance), reproductive rights, lesbian/gay rights, the elimination of racism and education discrimination in that regard, support of child-care programs, older women's economic protection, and support programs for women who have been victims of abuse.[69]

Objections to sexual harassment and violence inspired NOW's first Take Back the Night marches and enabled NOW to gain passage of federal legislation in 1994 aimed at stopping such violence.

Although NOW tends to be identified today primarily with the radical feminist programs of abortion "rights" and lesbian matters, it is difficult to deny the importance of NOW's efforts in connection with the overall improvement in the legal and economic status of women.

Feminists for Life of America

Feminists for Life of America was organized to voice the support of many feminists for the right of the unborn.[70] Feminists for Life represents women from all professions, religions, races, and socioeconomic backgrounds. Not only are Feminists for Life active in the support of life, as noted in their opposition to abortion, infanticide, capital punishment, and euthanasia, they are also committed to social change along these lines and active in the fight against gender-based violence.[71]

Feminists for Life work to dispel the myth that feminism has always stood for abortion: "[P]rominent early feminists advocated for greater female control over reproduction—but condemned the violence of abortion. In fact, Susan B. Anthony called it 'child murder.'"[72]

Other Feminist Groups

Other feminist organizations have been active in many areas of concern to women. For instance, "consciousness raising" groups promoted the development of the major writings and ideas on radical feminism.[73]

Other groups, such as the National Abortion Rights Action League (NARAL) and the National Women's Political Caucus (NWPC), have concentrated on a single issue in regard to the feminist movement. The League of Women Voters found favor with feminists as the group began to support feminist issues.[74]

Houston, Texas, hosted the Women's Year Conference (IWY) in 1977, which included twenty thousand observers and fifteen hundred delegates. Although 80 percent of the delegates represented a radical feminist agenda, some believe the conference led to the beginnings of the "pro-family" movement, as the remaining 20 percent of the women were in support of more traditional "family" values.[75]

The Equal Rights Amendment

The proposed *Equal Rights Amendment* (ERA) to the United States Constitution was heralded as a major step toward the institutionalization of women's rights. The ERA was ostensibly intended as a constitutional mandate that men and women should be treated equally by the state. Although the ERA failed to be adopted as a constitutional amendment, the debate led to the establishment of political structures and laws that continue today.

Eagle Forum/STOP ERA: Phyllis Schlafly

Phyllis Schlafly opposed NOW causes and, in particular, began STOP ERA to counter the efforts of the proposed constitutional amendment. Schlafly also began a second group, The Eagle Forum, in 1975. "Calling itself anti-ERA, anti-abortion, and profamily, this group chose the eagle as its symbol because it stood for traditional American values and because the eagle was one of the few creatures in society to have one mate for life."[76]

Schlafly led the fight against passage of the ERA, with the apparent objective of reinforcing the traditional role of women as being within the structure of marriage. Many credit Schlafly with the defeat of the ERA.

The Abortion Issue

Many feminists see abortion as being a key "right" that is necessary for them to live their lives on their own terms. Betty Friedan believed that "motherhood will only be a joyous and responsible human act when women are free to make, with full conscious choice and full human responsibility, the decisions to become mothers."[77]

Pro-abortion feminists and NOW members achieved much of the abortion rights agenda with the legalization of abortion by the United States Supreme Court in its landmark decision, *Roe v. Wade*.[78]

As a result, the abortion issue has resulted in untold carnage to the unborn, women, and families—and, indeed, the very moral structure of our society—and has divided the nation in a more corrosive way than the racial conflicts that preceded it in the civil rights movement.

The Lesbian View[79]

In the late 1970s, some in the women's liberation movement began to question the validity of heterosexuality itself.[80] Many believed that "it was lesbians who were most likely to focus personal attention and energy on women rather than on men."[81]

Some even believed that lesbians are the only true feminists because lesbian societies could not be based upon the oppression of women. Lesbianism evolved from a so-called sexual choice to a political one: women were choosing not to relate to men sexually or emotionally.

However, lesbianism has added to the extreme gender and sexual confusion that plagues modern culture. Sad to say, many children no longer have an idea what their sexual identity should be.

Because of the biological capability of a lesbian couple to reproduce, albeit only with the aid of technology, lesbianism challenges the very structure of Western culture, the traditional family unit.

Concerned Women for America

Concerned Women for America was founded in 1979 by Beverly LaHaye because she disagreed with the notion that NOW's Betty Friedan represented all American women. LaHaye believed that "the feminists' anti-God, anti-family rhetoric did not represent her beliefs, or those of the vast majority of women."[82]

CWA was first recognized as a small group of women working together to fight against the ERA, and it reports approximately fourteen hundred grassroots chapters, with members in all fifty states. While CWA's national office educates the grassroots chapters on pro-family issues and conducts lobbying efforts in the District of Columbia, local CWA members work in their communities to promote the sanctity of human life, encourage parental involvement in schools, oppose antifamily agendas, educate on the dangers of drugs and pornography, and support crisis pregnancy centers.[83]

Legal Issues

There are many legal issues that particularly affect women, perhaps especially *married* women and women with children. These involve the disposition of accumulated savings and retirement plans in the event of elderly divorce, provision and termination of health care and medical treatment, child day care, tax penalties and benefits, social welfare programs, custody, homeschool rights, spousal assault, rape, and even the matter of sexual relations. This book cannot cover all these issues. Thus, the following is a brief review of only the major issues affecting the rights and roles of women in modern America.

Abortion

The entrance of feminists into the abortion debate, classifying abortion as a "civil right," confused many women. Betty Friedan claimed that women's rights were the basis of the abortion movement. While speaking at the First National Conference for Repeal of Abortion Laws, Friedan declared abortion to be a basic inalienable right,[84] absent any concern for unborn life.

Parental Consent for Abortion for a Minor: In *Bellotti v. Baird,*[85] the United States Supreme Court held that parental consent requirements are permissible only with an extensive judicial bypass option. A pregnant minor may be required to obtain parental permission for an abortion as long as there is a procedure to bypass the parental consent requirement and to demonstrate to a judge that the minor is mature enough to make the decision alone or that an abortion would be in her best interests. Blanket parental consent requirements without a judicial bypass provision have been held to be unconstitutional.[86]

The Court's decision essentially strips from the familial realm the ability to deny the child's right to an abortion[87] and transports that decision to a detached judge.

Informed Consent Requirements: In *Planned Parenthood of Missouri v. Danforth,*[88] the Supreme Court construed "informed consent" to mean "the giving of information to the patient as to just what would be done and as to its consequences."[89] An informed consent provision was permitted because "the woman is the one primarily concerned, and her awareness of the decision and its significance may be assured, constitutionally, by the state to the extent of requiring her prior written consent."[90]

Casey and the Undue Burden Test: A landmark development in the abortion debate came in 1992 with the Supreme Court's decision in *Planned Parenthood of Southeastern Pennsylvania v. Casey,*[91] where the Court rejected the trimester framework of *Roe* as "unnecessary" and at times inconsistent with the "State's permissible exercise of its powers."[92] Reaffirming the basic holding of *Roe,* however, the Court embraced a new standard to determine whether abortion regulations were unconstitutional—the undue burden standard—and delineated new limitations on informed consent provisions. The state is permitted to require the "giving of truthful, nonmisleading information about the nature of the procedure, the attendant health risks and those of childbirth, and the 'probable gestational age' of the fetus."[93] In addition, the Court concluded that "informed choice need not be defined in such narrow terms that all considerations of the effect on the fetus are made irrelevant."[94] The state is permitted to "further its legitimate goal of protecting the life of the unborn by enacting legislation aimed at ensuring a decision that is mature and informed, even when in so doing the State expresses a preference for childbirth over abortion."[95]

Twenty-four-Hour Waiting Period: Prior to *Casey*, almost any restriction placed upon a woman's access to an abortion was unconstitutional. The *Casey* undue burden standard permits a state to enact "measures which favor childbirth over abortion, even if those measures do not further a health interest."[96] In *Casey*, the Court's plurality found that simply because the twenty-four-hour waiting period limited the doctor's discretion, the limitation was not, standing alone, enough reason to invalidate it: "The idea that important decisions will be more informed and deliberate if they follow some period of reflection does not strike us as unreasonable."[97] Concluding, the Court noted that "[e]ven the broadest reading of *Roe*, however, has not suggested that there is a constitutional right to abortion on demand."[98]

Spousal Consent Provisions: In *Danforth*,[99] Missouri required the consent of the woman's husband before an abortion would be authorized. Finding that this requirement was unconstitutional, the Supreme Court focused on the fact that if the decision of the husband differed from that of the wife, it was possible for only one of their decisions to prevail. Because it is the woman who bears the child and "is the more directly and immediately affected by the pregnancy, as between the two, the balance weighs in her favor."[100]

Later, in *Planned Parenthood of Southeastern Pennsylvania v. Casey*,[101] the Supreme Court delineated another reason for leaving the decision of abortion to the woman—the concern about domestic violence. Pennsylvania's abortion law prohibited a doctor from performing an abortion on a married woman unless the woman had a signed statement that she had notified her husband. The joint opinion relied on factual findings by the federal district trial court and on a body of research to conclude that most women who do not tell their husbands about an abortion have good reason for not doing so. According to the findings, many women are the victims of physical or psychological abuse by their husbands or are afraid of violence against themselves or their children if their husbands are opposed to the abortion. The Court's plurality seemed mainly concerned with the risks such a law would impose upon a battered wife. Pennsylvania's law was declared unconstitutional also because it was based on a traditional view of marriage "repugnant" to the Court's present understanding of marriage.[102]

Feminists and Abortion: Contrary to the views of many contemporary feminists, in the nineteenth century anti-abortion views were strongly held by the women's rights movement. This represents a key distinction between the historical women's rights movement, which argued for equal rights, and the modern feminist movement, which focuses entirely on the self-interest of women, even at the expense of unborn life and such societal institutions as the traditional family.

Nonetheless, many modern feminists oppose abortion. For example, Sidney Callahan has written various articles and books on the reason feminists should be opposed to abortion. She states:

> Faced with a choice between men and women, prolife feminists choose women, and faced with a conflict between women and the fetus, the choice is made for the fetus by analogous reasoning. In tragic conflicts and choices, one must give the benefit of the doubt to the more powerless and renounce solutions that do harm to human life.[103]

Abortion, however, remains the litmus test for many women in national politics. Indeed, few major women's political groups will support a woman who has doubts or reservations about *Roe v. Wade.* However, it is evident that the consequences of the Supreme Court's abortion decisions have led directly to the breakdown of societal values and to the absolute devaluation of human life.

Ironically, feminists label *Roe* as the case that liberated women from the oppression of men; however, *Roe* has also liberated men from "a sense of responsibility, from the pull of social bonds and the push of social pressures."[104]

RU 486: Hailed by the pro-choice community as a development that will make abortions more convenient, the drug RU 486 has been introduced into the United States for testing and eventual distribution.

RU 486 was first developed in France in 1982 and was lauded by pro-choice advocates as a revolution. However, according to a reporter who traveled to a French abortion clinic where the pill was being administered to women:

> [A]bortion carried out with RU 486 can be a lengthy "mini birth" process, sometimes with severe emotional consequences. Because a woman administers the drug to herself, it is a much more deliberate and conscious experience and is more likely to force a woman to confront her true feelings about her pregnancy and the moral dilemma of abortion. . . . [A] 1992 Swedish study found that women who had abor-

41

tions with RU 486 reported more pain, bleeding, and "moral consideration" than women who had surgical abortions.[105]

Although a 1992 survey showed that 78 percent of American women would prefer RU 486 to a surgical abortion,[106] most who have researched the effects of RU 486 would be surprised if the statistics were that high:

> [I]n Americans' eagerness to get the abortion pill, the psychological repercussions of this new procedure have been largely overlooked. The magic pill appears to have an unexpected power. It provides a dim mirror in which women may confront, for better or for worse, the reality of what they are doing.[107]

Women in Combat

A continuing controversy for modern feminists and others involves women in combat. Many see the debate as a conflict between the nation's concern for security and the feminists' concern for equal treatment under the laws.

The Supreme Court has made various pronouncements on the special status of the military. The military is a "specialized community governed by separate discipline from that of the civilian"[108] and "has developed laws and traditions of its own during its long history."[109]

Even though the military is not exempt from constitutional review, constitutional rights are applied with great deference to the needs of the military.[110] The constitutional rights of individual service members are viewed as subordinate to the military's need for "instinctive obedience, unity, commitment, and esprit de corps."[111] "The military system categorizes, classifies, and rationalizes in ways that would not be tolerated in the civilian sector under principles of equal protection or anti-discrimination statutes."[112]

Because Congress has permitted the armed forces to establish their own definitions of combat, the statutory language does not reveal the meaning of the combat exclusion. The Gulf War provided the impetus for partial repeal of combat exclusion laws. Approximately thirty-five thousand women served in the war—with eleven killed and two taken prisoner.

In 1993, Congress repealed the law exempting women from service on combatant ships. Early in 1994, then Defense Secretary Les Aspin announced a redefinition of "direct ground combat," along with repeal of the Risk Rule. Under the new policy, women will be excluded only from units intended primarily to engage in direct combat, which is defined as "engaging an enemy on the ground with . . . weapons, while being exposed to hostile fire and to a high probability of direct physical contact with enemy troops."[113]

As a result, women may now enter specialties that involve extraordinary physical strength or a high risk of injury or capture. All the armed forces were ordered to lift restrictions on women flying combat aircraft. However, there are only about eight hundred female pilots in uniform—out of more than forty-one thousand pilots in all the services.[114]

The issue of women in combat is still not entirely resolved. Before Secretary Aspin's order, about half of the 1.75 million positions in the armed forces were closed to the 201,000 women in uniform because they could not serve in combat units. Under the new rules, women are still ineligible for 40 percent of the positions. This is because those assignments are in "combat arms" of army and marine ground forces, mainly infantry, armored units, and artillery.[115]

Workplace Issues

Equality in the workplace remains a major issue, even though two of every three new workers are women, and women now comprise almost 45 percent of the labor force, with 56 million female workers. Some 60 percent of the mothers with children under age six are in the workforce; 75 percent with children aged 6–17 now work, up from 39 percent in 1960; and approximately 14.2 percent of families have a wife who stays home full-time to rear the children.[116]

There are signs, however, which show that some women are leaving the workforce to return home. Richard Hokenson, chief economist for Donaldson, Lufkin and Jenrette Securities in New York, released a study in 1993 which indicated that women of childbearing age have been leaving their jobs and returning home in significant numbers.[117]

Analysts have offered various explanations for the change. First, many are finding that time with children is a higher priority than outside employment. Second, the cost of high-quality child care is high. About 80 percent of a working mother's paycheck goes to support her children, with child care the major cost.[118] Third, increasing dissatisfaction with public education, coupled with an inability to afford private schooling, results in more mothers staying home to educate their children.[119]

Maternity Leave

Pregnancy on the job is not unusual: 85 percent of working women will become pregnant at some point in their careers.[120] Various federal, state, and local provisions protect women's jobs when they decide to have a child. For example, the 1978 Federal Pregnancy Discrimination Act provides that employers cannot refuse to hire a woman simply because she is pregnant, fire her because she is pregnant, force her to go on leave at some arbitrary point in her pregnancy, require that she take a set amount of time off after the baby is born, or penalize her by reducing the benefits she has earned.[121] The Act covers private employers, state and local governments, educational institutions with fifteen or more employees, all private and public employment agencies, labor organizations, and joint labor-management committees for apprentice and training programs.

However, if a woman's pregnancy would prevent her from doing her job, she may be denied employment. This law does not require an employer to give the employee any specific amount of time off for maternity leave, nor does it require the employer to establish any special benefits for other workers where none exist. These issues are covered by the Family and Medical Leave Act of 1993.[122]

Under the 1978 Act, women who are pregnant or have recently given birth must be treated the same as other temporarily disabled employees for all employment-related purposes, including fringe benefits and insurance.

The Family and Medical
Leave Act of 1993

In 1993, President Bill Clinton signed into law the Family and Medical Leave Act (FMLA),[123] which required businesses with fifty or more employees to provide at least twelve weeks of unpaid leave for the birth or adoption of a child; to care for a spouse, child, or parent with a serious illness; or because the employee is seriously ill and unable to work. Employees who take this leave are entitled to resume work at their former position or an equivalent position upon their return.

A 1988 study by the Institute for Women's Policy Research estimated that working women lose $31 billion a year because of lost wages, experience, and seniority associated with having children.[124] Although there was much initial opposition to the Act by businesses, a Conference Board study discovered that most companies find it relatively easy to comply with the FMLA.[125] A 1988 Cornell survey of leave policies among businesses with fifty or more employees estimated that mandated family and medical leave would save the jobs of 150,000 workers a year who otherwise would have to quit their jobs due to a temporary health crisis, saving businesses $244 million a year in employee turnover expenses.[126]

Equal Employment

Women are sometimes discriminated against in employment because of their gender. Even where women are hired, they often remain below management levels because of the infamous "glass ceiling." However, various federal provisions prohibit discrimination by employers on the basis of sex.[127]

Title VII of the Civil Rights Act of 1964 bans discriminatory practices in all aspects of the employment relationship by covered employers, unions, and employment agencies.[128] Its goal is to equalize the opportunities provided to all protected groups. This encompasses not only hiring and firing but also compensation and the terms, conditions, and privileges of employment.[129]

Equal Pay

The wage gap between men and women is still a problem. The average working woman earns only seventy-one cents for every dollar paid to her male counterpart.[130] The Equal Pay Act of 1963[131] spells out federal equal pay requirements.

Three factors are to be used in making comparisons of jobs held by males and females: equal work; performance requiring equal skill, effort, and responsibilities; and similar working conditions.[132] The Act specifically exempts payments made under a pay system based on either seniority, merit, quality or quantity of production, or on any other factor other than sex.[133]

Because the Equal Pay Act only makes it illegal to pay men and women differently for doing the same job, it has not contributed much to closing the wage gap. Some contend that this is because men and women do not do the same kind of work. Approximately 80 percent of women are in traditionally female job categories, such as waitressing, sales, and clerical work.[134]

Conclusion

It seems clear that much is yet to be done respecting women and their rightful place in American society. Legal and discriminatory practices must be eliminated. However, the very real differences between women and men created by God must not be ignored in the process.

Denying the differences between women and men reduces the value of each. Jesus Christ provided the answer nearly two thousand years ago. Christians, therefore, are not merely uniquely equipped to resolve the problems surrounding the rights and roles of women: They have a mandate to do so.

Notes

1. Gabriele Dietze, in Bonnie S. Anderson and Judith P. Zinsser, *A History of Their Own: Women in Europe from Prehistory to the Present* (New York: Harper & Row, 1988), 2:426–27 (citation omitted).

2. Barbara Ehrenreich, "Susan Smith: Corrupted by Love?" *Time*, 7 August 1995, 78.

3. *See generally* Anderson and Zinsser, *A History of Their Own*, vol. 2.

4. *American Women in the Nineties: Today's Critical Issues*, ed. Sherie Matteo (Boston: Northeastern Univ. Press, 1993), 126.

5. It is interesting that few appear to question whether a man works as a matter of choice or economic necessity. One could safely assume that the conditioning of society implies both insofar as men are concerned. The dilemma faced by women in this regard is, however, being extended to men who want to trade a decrease in professional success for more time with their families. Contemporary corporate America, as well as the people in it, remains uncertain as to how to respond to such demands.

6. Ben Witherington III, *Women and the Genesis of Christianity* (Cambridge: Cambridge Univ. Press, 1990), 3–9.

7. Jean Bethke Elshtain, *Public Man, Private Woman* (Princeton, N.J.: Princeton Univ. Press, 1981), 74–80, 84.

8. The term used to denote use of the male as the norm is *androcentrism*.

9. The failure to distinguish between respect for and obliteration of differences is a key weakness in today's political correctness and so-called diversity and multicultural initiatives which require that all differences be viewed as of no import.

10. Genesis 1:27 (italics added).

11. Matthew 19:4–5; *cf.* Genesis 2:24.

12. Rachel Conrad Wahlberg, *Jesus and the Freed Woman* (New York: Paulist, 1978), 76.

13. Heinrich Böll, quoted in Elisabeth Moltmann-Wendel, *The Women Around Jesus: Reflections on Authentic Personhood* (London: SCM, 1982), 94.

14. *See* Luke 6:1–2.

15. Luke 8:1–3.

16. John 11:1–5.

17. Witherington, *Women and the Genesis of Christianity*, 99.

18. Luke 10:38–42.

19. John 11:1–44.

20. John 12:1–8. *See* Evelyn and Frank Stagg, *Women in the World of Jesus* (Philadelphia: Westminster, 1978), 117.

21. Luke 10:39.

22. Luke 10:41–42.

23. Stagg, *Women in the World of Jesus*, 118.

24. *Ibid.*

25. *Ibid.*, 119.

26. John 11:27.

27. *See* Matthew 16:16.

28. Witherington, *Women and the Genesis of Christianity*, 106.

29. John 12:1–8.

30. Moltmann-Wendel, *The Women Around Jesus*, 57.

31. *Ibid.*, 55.

32. Witherington, *Women and the Genesis of Christianity*, 109.

33. Moltmann-Wendel, *The Women Around Jesus*, 95.

34. John 13:13–15.

35. Luke 22:27.

36. According to one author, the view that John said Jews have no dealings with Samaritans is a mistranslation of the Greek; in reality, John's statement was to the effect that Jews do not use vessels with Samaritans, referring to the code of purity. Stagg, *Women in the World of Jesus*, 116.

37. *Ibid.*

38. John 4:27.

39. Wahlberg, *Jesus and the Freed Woman*, 6.

40. John 4:16–18.

41. Witherington, *Women and the Genesis of Christianity*, 71.

42. *See* Luke 15:1–2.

43. John 4:42.

44. Stagg, *Women in the World of Jesus*, 117.

45. Luke 13:10–17.

46. John 8:1–11.

47. John 8:6.

48. John 8:11.

49. Stagg, *Women in the World of Jesus*, 112.

50. *Ibid.*, 113.

51. *Ibid.*

52. *Ibid.*

53. Luke 13:12.

54. Stagg, *Women in the World of Jesus*, 106.

55. Richard M. Pope, *The Church and Its Culture* (St. Louis: Bethany, 1965), 276.

56. Thomas Aquinas, *Summa Theologiae*, Q. 92, Art. 1.

57. *Ibid.*, Q. 98, Art. 2.

58. "General information about NOW," NETSCAPE.

59. Barbara Ryan, *Feminism and the Women's Movement* (New York, London: Routledge, 1992), 85, in reference to an interview with Carol King, Regional NOW representative (July 1983).

60. Irene Stuber, "July 26, 1995 Episode 362 Women of Achievement and Herstory," *Women of Achievement and Herstory*, NETSCAPE.

61. Pat Schroeder, *Champion of the Great American Family* (New York: Random, 1989), 21.

62. Betty Friedan, *It Changed My Life: Writings on the Women's Movement* (New York: Random, 1963), 63.

63. *Ibid.*, 20–27.

64. *Ibid.*, 35–42.

65. *Ibid.*, 83.

66. *Ibid.*, 84.

67. "The History of the National Organization for Women," NETSCAPE.

68. NOW's litigation efforts were important in the struggle for equal access to well-paying jobs. For example, NOW's *Weeks v. Southern Bell* case resulted in the Fifth Circuit Court of Appeals ruling that it was a violation of Title VII of the Civil Rights Act to bar women from jobs that involved lifting more than thirty pounds. "The History of the National Organization for Women," NETSCAPE.

69. "General Information about NOW," NETSCAPE.

70. "If you think real feminists can't be pro-life . . . think again," NETSCAPE.

71. *Ibid.*

72. *See ibid.*

73. Ryan, *Feminism and the Women's Movement*, 47.

74. *Ibid.*, 67. In support of a "women only" membership with the league, Gloria Steinem, a leading feminist and editor/founder of *Ms.* magazine, said: "We cannot integrate with men on an equal basis until we are equal. If you admit men, let them do the typing, run the child care centers and donate money." *Ibid.*, 59; *see also* chapter 5. (Since that time, the league has admitted male members.)

75. *Ibid.*, 75.

76. Ryan, *Feminism and the Women's Movement*, 69, in reference to Fishman and Fuller, 1981.

77. Friedan, *It Changed My Life*, 125.

78. 410 U.S. 113 (1973).

79. A feminist lesbian group, the Radicalesbians, described the word *lesbian* as a "label invented by the Man to throw at any woman who dares to be his equal, who dares to challenge his prerogatives." Hester Eisenstein, *Contemporary Feminist Thought* (Boston: Hall, 1983), 50. As

quoted from "The Woman-Identified Woman," in *Radical Feminism*, ed. Koedt et al., 240–45.

80. *See* Sasha Gregory Lewis, *Sunday's Women: A Report on Lesbian Life Today* (Boston: Beacon, 1979), 158.

81. Eisenstein, *Contemporary Feminist Thought*, 48.

82. *See* Concerned Women for America's brochure.

83. *See* Concerned Women for America's *FACT SHEET.*

84. Friedan, *It Changed My Life*, 124.

85. *Bellotti v. Baird*, 443 U.S. 622 (1979).

86. *H.L. v. Matheson*, 450 U.S. 398 (1981). Justice White, dissenting in *Bellotti*, expressed his incredulity at the majority's opinion:

> [T]he Court now holds it unconstitutional for a state to require that in all cases parents receive notice that their daughter seeks an abortion and, if they object to the abortion, an opportunity to participate in a hearing that will determine whether it is in the "best interests" of the child to undergo the surgery. Until now, I would have thought inconceivable a holding that the United States Constitution forbids even notice to parents when their minor child who seeks surgery objects to such notice and is able to convince a judge that the parents should be denied participation in the decision.

Bellotti, 443 U.S. at 657 (White, J., dissenting).

87. *See* John W. Whitehead, *Religious Apartheid* (Chicago: Moody, 1994), 90.

88. *Planned Parenthood of Missouri v. Danforth*, 428 U.S. 52, 67 (1976).

89. *Id.*

90. *Id.*

91. *Planned Parenthood of Southeastern Pennsylvania v. Casey*, 112 S.Ct. 2818 (1992).

92. *Id.*

93. *Id.* at 2823.

94. *Id.* at 2823–24.

95. *Id.* at 2824.

96. *Id.* at 2825.

97. *Id.*

98. *Id.* at 2826.

99. *Planned Parenthood of Missouri v. Danforth,* 428 U.S. 52.

100. *Id.* at 71.

101. *Casey,* 112 St.Ct. at 2818.

102. *Id.* at 2831.

103. "Value Choices in Abortion," *Abortion: Understanding Differences,* ed. Sidney Callahan (New York, London: Plenum, 1984), 296–97.

104. *Ibid.*

105. Louise Levathes, "Listening to RU 486," *Health,* January/February 1995, 87.

106. Lauren Picker, "Abortion to Go?" *Bazaar,* October 1994, 246, 247–48.

107. Levathes, "Listening to RU 486," 89.

108. *Orloff v. Willoughby,* 345 U.S. 83, 94, *reh'g denied,* 345 U.S. 931 (1953).

109. *Parker v. Levy,* 417 U.S. 733, 743 (1974).

110. *Id.* at 758.

111. *Goldman v. Weinberger,* 475 U.S. 503, 507 (1986).

112. Lucy V. Katz, "Free a Man to Fight: The Exclusion of Women from Combat Positions in the Armed Forces," 10 *Law and Inequality* 1, 4 (1991).

113. *Congressional Quarterly,* "Aspin Opens Billets to Women," 15 January 1994, 78.

114. Bruce W. Nelan, "Annie Get Your Gun," *Time,* 10 May 1993, 42, 43.

115. *Ibid.,* 43. Many argue that women should be excluded from combat because women are not as physically able to handle combat as men. They mention the rigor-

ous routine and basic training that combat troops must withstand in order to be effective on the battlefield.

However, most proponents of women in combat do not advocate lowering the physical requirements; rather, they simply request that women be given the chance to meet the same physical requirements the men must meet. In fact, proponents of women in combat concede that most women will not be able to pass the rigorous test but think that this is no reason to ban all women *per se*.

Although proponents of women in combat contend that the advancement of technology results in a diminished need for physical strength and stamina, most say that combat is no more refined, no less barbaric, and no less physically demanding than it has historically been. Army Lt. Gen. J. H. Binford Peay III, now commander-in-chief of the Central Command, said: "In fact, technology has made today's battlefield a more lethal, violent, shocking and horrific place than it has ever been." Elaine Donnelly, "Unit Cohesion vs. 'Career Advancement': Should Women Serve in Ground Combat Arms?," *VFW*, February 1995, 28.

Desert Storm, which differed in many ways from most wars in American history, created the illusion that modern warfare is a "high-tech computer game [which is] relatively easy and risk-free." *Ibid.*, 29.

Opposition to repeal is also founded on the idea that men, when fighting alongside women, will have a natural tendency to protect the women from danger, rather than the two working together as a team to fight the enemy. This argument seems to be nothing more than mere speculation because civilian men and women have shown great competency when forced to work together in dangerous situations. For example, policemen and women are often paired together on patrol. However, Commissioner Kate O'Beirne contends that allowing women to engage in combat would erode American cultural values. She says: "Right now, millions of American mothers are raising their sons to protect and defend women. Neither men nor women should be required, as the price of equality, to sacrifice this fundamental principle that governs a civilized order." *Ibid.*, 29–30.

Some think that society will be less able to handle female casualties than male casualties. Instructors at the Survival, Evasion, Resistance and Escape (SERE) training center note: "If a policy change is made, and women are allowed into combat positions, there must be a concerted effort to educate the American public on the increased likelihood that women will be raped, will come home in bodybags, and will be exploited." *Ibid.*, 29.

Most do not rely on this as the sole reason for maintaining the combat exclusion because this implies that women's lives are more important to society than men's.

A more controversial reason for maintaining the combat exclusion is that women prisoners of war will be a threat to national security because they will not be able to withstand punishment. Those who cite this as their reason for supporting the combat exclusion do so even though history shows that women prisoners of war were able to withstand harsh treatment. They claim that the women taken as prisoners of war in World War II were nurses and laundry maids, not combatants. If women combatants were taken as prisoners, the enemy would treat the women with no respect to their gender. However, those who claim that women would be unable to undergo torture without giving away secret information undermine the extent of their allegiance to their country and imply that men have a greater level of allegiance.

Some contend that allowing women to engage in combat will result in the deterioration of the family. The mother, as the primary caregiver, will be absent from home, and the care of the children will be left to the father who, in most situations, has less time for the family. However, this argument does not directly address the issue of women in combat; rather, it simply opposes women in the military. Just because the combat position is opened to women does not necessarily mean that more women will end up enlisting in the military. In fact, it will mean that women who are already enlisted in the military will move up from noncombat positions to those involving direct combat.

Another argument that fails because it does not directly address the issue of women in combat is the contention that women will become pregnant when integrated with the male troops. This argument does not address the point, for women already share the same barracks with men. Even if women continue to be excluded from combat, pregnancies will result because women and men reside in the same barracks. However, the argument that pregnant women will hinder the effectiveness of the military could have some merit.

Male bonding is an important part of troop cohesion and unity of troops. If women are permitted to assume combat positions, this essential element will likely be lost. Some argue that this will not be the result because females are experts at communication and will be an asset to troop cohesion. However, Dr.

David Marlowe, chief of military psychiatry at Reed Army Hospital, points out that "military bonding is not just friendship or enjoying one another's company; there must be an element of reciprocity. 'You cover me; I cover you. You must have the skills to keep me alive, and I must have the skills to keep you alive.'" Donnelly, "Unit Cohesion vs. 'Career Advancement,'" 30.

Finally, opponents of women in combat argue that women are nurturers and are, by nature, incapable of assuming a killer-like mentality on the battlefield. Peter instructs women on how they are to act: "[L]et it be the hidden person of the heart, with the incorruptible ornament of a gentle and quiet spirit, which is very precious in the sight of God." 1 Peter 3:4. Warfare seems antithetical to the gentle and quiet spirit women are instructed to have.

Surprisingly, army women are somewhat apprehensive about women in combat roles. A 1992 survey found that only 4 percent of enlisted women and 11 percent of female officers said they would volunteer for combat duty. Moskos, "Mandating Inclusion," 24. However, both feminists and women in the army agree that the categorical exclusion of women from direct combat roles is a limit on full citizenship. Representative Patricia Schroeder (D.-Colo.) claimed that if women were allowed to participate in combat, sexual harassment would decline. However, sexual harassment is apparently the most common in the Coast Guard, the only service with no gender restrictions. *Ibid.*, 25.

116. General Accounting Office, *The Changing Workforce: Demographic Issues Facing the Federal Government* (Washington, D.C.: GAO, 1992).

117. Leith Anderson, "Clocking Out," *Christianity Today*, 12 September 1994, 30.

118. *Ibid.*

119. *Ibid.*, 31.

120. U.S. Dept. of Labor, *Labor Force Participation Unchanged Among Mothers with Young Children, News,* 88 (September 1988), 431.

121. 49 U.S.C.A. 2000e(k) (West 1994).

122. 29 U.S.C.A., 2601 (West 1995 Supp.).

123. Armond D. Budish, "Your Family or Your Job: You Don't Have to Choose?" *Family Circle,* 11 January 1994, 140.

124. R. Spalter-Roth and H. Hartmann, *Unnecessary Losses: Costs to Americans of the Lack of Family and Medical Leave* (Washington, D.C.: Institute for Women's Policy Research, 1988).

125. *HR Focus,* "FMLA Compliance Proves Easier than Expected," April 1995, 14.

126. E. Trzcinski and W. T. Alpert, "Job Guaranteed Medical Leave: Reducing Termination Costs to Businesses," paper presented at the 1992 World Congress on the Family, Columbus, Ohio, August 1992.

127. *See* John W. Whitehead, *Censored on the Job* (Chicago: Moody, 1995).

128. 42 U.S.C.A. 2000e (West 1994).

129. In addition, in 1967 Executive Order 11375 extended the ban on discrimination on the basis of gender by federal contractors doing $10,000 or more of government business that the president had applied in 1965 to race, color, religion, and national origin. This amended order prohibits discrimination and requires affirmative action to ensure nondiscrimination in "[r]ates of pay or any other forms of compensation." Mitchell Meyer, *Women and Employee Benefits* (New York: The Conference Board, 1978), 26.

130. Maud Lavin, "Waging War on Wages," *New Woman,* February 1995, 126.

131. 29 U.S.C.A. 206 (West 1978).

132. Meyer, *Women and Employee Benefits*, 25.

133. 29 U.S.C.A. 206 (West 1978).

134. Lavin, "Waging War on Wages," 128.